Rollo and Ruff

And the Little Fluffy Bird

Mick Inkpen

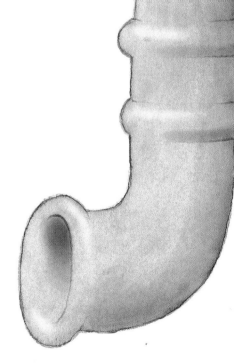

Hodder
Children's
Books

A division of Hachette Children's Books

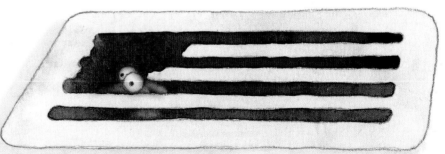

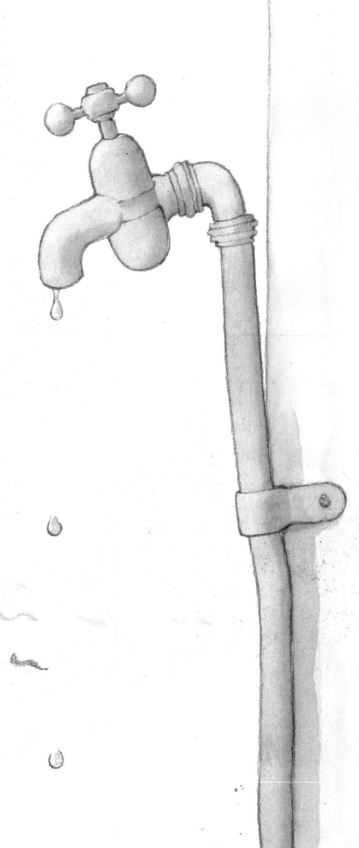

Rollo is on his
mat, in the yard,
behind the Cornershop.
The sun dawdles
into the sky.
The yard tap drips.

Plink.

Plink.

Plink.

Along comes the LFB
with some plastic string.
The LFB is always on
the lookout for things to
add to her nest.
'Hello LFB!'
(Little Fluffy Bird, in case you were wondering).

It is a normal Tuesday...

E xcept it isn't.
   Lately strange things have
been happening.
   In the night something has
chewed Rollo's mat...

And this morning
his little red ball
is missing.
  'LFB, have you been
pecking my mat?'
  The LFB is too busy
to answer. She has
found a feather and a
twig to go with her bit
of plastic string.

There are bits of Rollo's
mat all over the yard.
And something else.
   Little red bits.
Little red bits?
   Bits of his little red ball!

   And that's not all.
There are footprints...
   wet footprints...

. . .but whose footprints?

'Rollo, come quickly!'
It is the LFB.
She is so excited she can
   hardly speak!
'There's something asleep
   in my nest!'
It is true.
   There is a little,
pink tail.

The creature is
thin and scruffy and
twitches in its sleep.
   It is clutching what is
left of Rollo's little
   red ball.
'What is it?'
   whispers the LFB.
'I don't know,'
   whispers Rollo.
He sniffs the air.
   'But whatever it is,
it's a bit...
            stinky!'

   The creature opens
an eye...

...and gives a terrified

Squeak!

It jumps out of the nest,
scampers across the yard
and disappears down
the drain. **Plop!**

There it stays,
blinking in the dark.

'**W**hat are you?'
says Rollo.
'And why have you
been eating my ball?'
There is a long silence.
Then suddenly...

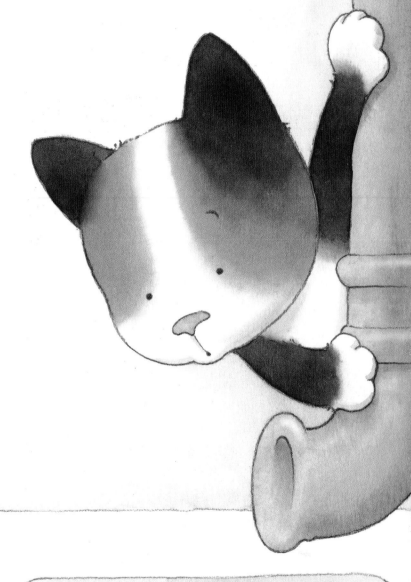

I didn't mean to... I couldn't help it... I was hungry... I was starving! You just couldn't imagine what the other rats eat... Horrible things! Slimy things! Slippery things! Sticky things! Wriggly things! Disgusting oozy things! Things that

have gone green! Things that have gone furry! I can't eat oozy, green, furry things!

And the little rat begins to cry. 'My name is **Ruff**,' it sniffs. 'Am I really **stinky?**'

For ages the little rat won't come out of the drain.

So Rollo brings some sweeties from the Cornershop. He lays them in a long line.

Soon a pointy, whiskery nose is sniffing the air. And not long after out comes...

. . .Ruff.

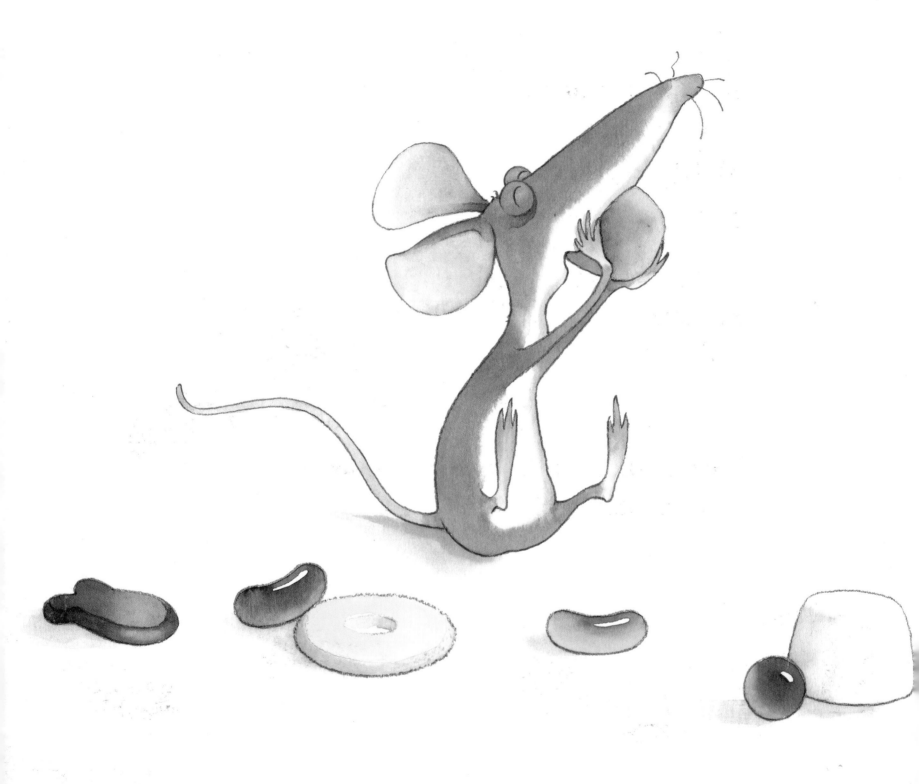

R uff has never
tasted anything
so lovely!
So fantastic!
So delicious!
He eats
the lot.

Then he falls asleep with his cheeks
full of marshmallows.

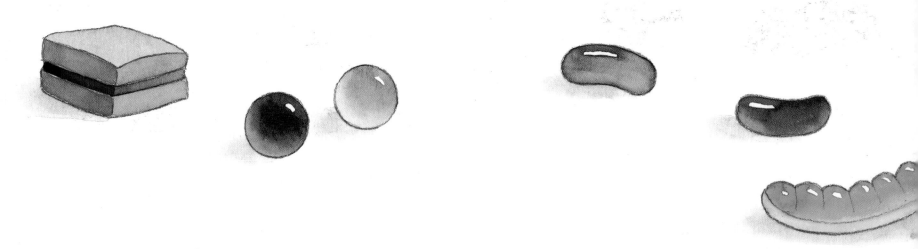

Ruff is dreaming
of sweeties,
and the LFB is
whispering something
in Rollo's ear.
She has a plan.

'**Y**es! Yes!'
says Rollo,
'We can use this!'
He pulls pieces
out of his mat,
while the LFB flies
back and forth,
carrying them away
in her beak.

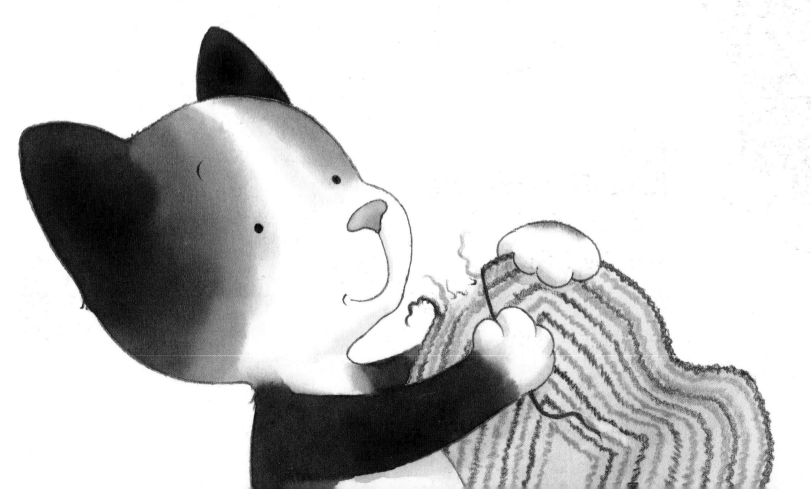

Rollo wakes Ruff.
'Ruff! This is your
new front door!'
But Ruff looks
confused.
Sleepily he climbs
back into the drain.
'No! No! No! Ruff!
Not down the drain!
Go up!
Go up!
Go up
the pipe!'

So here
is Ruff,
climbing
up out
of the
dark,
up
towards
the roof,
and
out . . .

. . .under the
wide sky,
 where there are
a billion stars
 twinkling,
and a nest made
 out of Rollo's mat
  just for him.

Here he lies,
feeling full,
and warm,
and safe,
and ...happy.

'Goodnight Ruff.'
It is Rollo's voice
echoing up the
drainpipe...

'Goodnight Rollo.'

Squeak.

Squeak.

Squeak.

Squeak.

Squeak.

Squeak.

Squeak.

It is the sound
 of the cat flap
swinging on the
 back door of the
Cornershop.
 Everyone has gone
to bed.

Nobody sees Ruff
 come back down
the drainpipe
 and creep
across the
 yard...

Plink.

Plink.
Plink.
The yard tap drips.
Splish.
Splash.
Splish.
It is Ruff
making sure
that nobody
will **ever**
call him
stinky
again.